DESERT FLOWERS

Poems of Love and Life

Expressions From a Military Wife

MARGARET ROBERTS

Published by Hub House Publishing
7431 S. Ireland Circle, Suite B
Centennial, Colorado 80016
info@hubhousepublishing.com
www.hubhousepublishing.com

ISBN-10: 0-9789904-2-0

ISBN-13: 978-0-9789904-2-8

Library of Congress Control Number: 2008907319

Cover Design Concept: Velia Hall

Cover Design and Interior Layout: Ronda Taylor, Taylor by Design

For

Bobbie

Lizzie Bear

Lucy

Horatio

Testimonials

What others are saying about this book . . .

"Reading these passages brought back a flow of memories. Thanks for allowing me to revisit my past."

— Patricia Hester Connor,
proud daughter of a retired Air Force Staff Sergeant

"Margaret Roberts has redefined the meaning of a "military wife" adding richness, beauty, and dimension through an anthology of poems with some luminous moments."

— Major and Mrs. Chris Gologanoff, USMC Retired

"Wow! As the wife of a retired soldier, this book touched my heart. It is an inspirational read. Kudos to the author."

— Mirna Michel, Army Wife

"It surrounds the heart with memories; it captures the heart and soul of an old soldier. In a silent whisper it says, "Yes," we have taken that journey."

— LTC and Mrs. Frank Saunders, U.S. Army Retired

Acknowledgments

Thank you to my friends who supported me in this effort: Liz Anthony, C.J. Buckley, Pat Connors, Doris Harkleroad, Denise Holdridge, Sylvia Johnson, Yvette Mason, Tisa Mitchell, Traci Parker, Sylvia Pate, Lisa Wilson, Pam Wilson, Billie Van Horn, Teresa Dunkle, Adele Hodges, Rhonda Lattimore, Lucinda Cleveland, Jeanne Rosenthal, Desnee Young, and Sharon Wilson.

Thank you Mark and Michelle Lewis for your encouragement, and heartfelt gratitude to the Reddick and Roberts families for their support. To S.F. Young, Jerry Young, Sandra Yarborough and Ed Dixon, your continued support of my projects over the years is appreciated.

The administrative and organizational skills of Lisa McElwee have been invaluable to the completion of this project; I extend sincere gratitude to her. To the Unity House Publishing staff for maintaining confidence in my ability and The Red Pen Editor for her discerning eye.

To my husband, Alex, who made it possible for me to blossom as a member of the military family, my deepest appreciation and love always.

Contents

Introduction

Nothing is more delicate or more beautiful than a blanket of desert flowers. Yellow, purple, red, blue, and white flowers growing as far as the eye can see. Flowers displaying a beauty that cannot be measured or explained, covering what seems to be dead, dry, infertile soil.

Let's compare these flowers to the military family experience. Separation from loved ones, friends and things familiar are the norm, often giving a sense of isolation in a harsh environment. But as the desert brings forth beautiful flowers, so the military family blossoms, especially military wives.

Military wives are caring, committed, "flowers," living in a world often misunderstood by those not directly associated with military life. These brave, spiritual "flowers" are the cohesive element that keep the military family experience strong and vital.

This book of poems is a tribute to the military family experience, and is especially dedicated to the "desert flowers" all over the world who are married to members who serve, or have served, in the United States Armed Forces. It is a tribute to the uniqueness of the military lifestyle. This book would not be possible without the love and support of the following military wives who have played a pivotal role in my life: Ginny Cisneros, Val Dandridge, Audrey Gillick, Vern Guidry, Cookie Ivory, Vicki Johnson, Dee McCloskey, Suzanne Palm, Lou Reid, Elfreda Saunders, and Roz Stanley.

— Margaret Roberts

DESERT FLOWERS

Poems of Love and Life

WE ARE THE ONES

We are the men and women who stand tall for America.
We took an oath to honor and defend
your rights whenever and wherever called.

We are the men and women who risk our
well being so you can play, work, learn, sleep,
dream and live in peace, harmony and freedom.

We are the men and women who ask to be
kept in your hearts, minds and prayers.
We are the ones who sometimes give our lives for yours.

THE MILITARY WIFE

Have you ever thought about the world of a military wife?
Are you amused by the regimentation of her life?

Are you puzzled by the way she seems so calm
When her warrior is surely facing harm?

Does her unique lifestyle ever make you pause
To wonder if there is a deeper cause
That makes her stay on course when times are rough
That keeps her brave and strong when life gets tough.

There's really no mystique about her ways
She does what's needed to get through each new day
She's charged with keeping the home front intact
Until her weary warrior comes safely back.

A DESERT FLOWER

I am a desert flower laughing in the sun.
The sand surrounds my world as I watch coyotes run.

It is a miracle I exist in such hostile terrain.
But thanks to Mother Nature I survive on little rain.

Amid the sagebrush, rocks, and sand
I proudly claim my place.

I am a desert flower, part of God's vast desert space.

LIKE THE DESERT FLOWER

They stand tall.

They are united in a wonderful array of hues
bursting from the desert sand
as if a mirage.

How do they thrive in such infertile ground?
How do they keep their radiant beauty
under the fierce desert sun?
What is the secret to their survival?

A vibrant array emerged in a lifestyle that is
unpredictable, yet exciting.

How do they thrive in a world of such
uncertainty and constant change?

How do they keep their radiant beauty
during time of war and separation
from loved ones?

What is the secret to the military wife's survival?

Just like the desert flowers
military wives are extraordinary mysteries of God.

BLOSSOM ONCE AGAIN

There is a dryness in the air
as dry as the parched desert floor.
There is harshness to this world
that eagles see as they soar.

But when the winter rains soak the desert sand
Beautiful spring flowers blanket the once barren land.

There is a sadness in their eyes
as they watch the Marines leave.
There will be loneliness in their world
that only time can relieve.

But when the winter rains soak the desert sand
Beautiful spring flowers blanket the once barren land.

There is joy in their hearts
tears stream down their faces.
The Marines return from
far away places.

As the winter rain soaks the desert sand
the Marine wives will blossom once again.

THE KISS

The dress is perfectly tailored as if created solely for her.
Her hair is stylishly coiffed, highlights sparkle in the sun.
Today she must look perfect to greet her Marine
who has been away too long.

As his vehicle approaches the base,
he can visualize her beauty.
He knows she will be waiting for him
as she has many years before.
Today he must make her proud to greet him
for he has been away too long.

Their eyes lock as they quickly run to meet.
Six months of being apart, erased in a single embrace.
Their lips meet and her knees go weak.
He holds her so tightly that her heart skips a beat.

The kiss is a heavenly beginning for those
who have been apart too long.

CHAPEL CALL

The one God and Father of us all
Asks if you hear the chapel call.
No excuses from you or me
You just have to go
The cost is free.

The chaplains are trained in your religion of choice
Go to the chapel and hear God's voice.
The praying and preaching and praising in song
Won't take much time
The service isn't long.

If you go to the chapel there's one guarantee
You'll make a friend in Jesus while down on your knees.
You'll even learn how to pray your troubles away
You'll be uplifted in many ways.

So heed God's call and go hear His word
You may hear something you've never heard.
You'll be surprised at who you'll see
You just have to go
The cost is free.

BROKEN HEARTED

The realization that we're not going to make it
is hard to accept.

Deep in my soul I long for days gone by
when our love seemed enough.

The military lifestyle is too uncertain
and the long absences are unbearable.

My love of adventure has been replaced
with a longing for stability.

Your world is no longer mine.

We wanted our love to last.

We are left broken hearted.

THROUGH THE EYES OF A WIFE

Your vigor and vitality will never fade
You will always be strong and brave
You will always be a protector
Your youth will live forever
Through the eyes of a wife.

Your tenderness as a father
Your gentleness as a lover
Your willingness to help others
Your love for your family
Will forever be seen
Through the eyes of a wife.

Your erect stance and commanding voice
Your ability to lead others
Your strong body and sound mind
Your sense of humor and pensive moods
Will remain
Through the eyes of a wife.

You may be older, your hair more gray
A bit slower in your stride
You remain combat ready
The uniform can still be worn
Through the eyes of a wife.

GOOD-BYE MAMA

BUT MAMA,

I love him. He is brave and strong and
so handsome in his uniform.

YES MAMA,

I know. I'll be far from home and family,
but most of all, far from you.

NO MAMA,

I don't know. We'll go from place to place,
never knowing how long we'll stay.

OH MAMA,

He loves me. He will protect and care
for me as a husband should.

PLEASE MAMA,

Be happy. Be happy for me and think of me always.

WELL MAMA,

I'll miss you. I'll remember all you taught me.

GOOD-BYE MAMA,

I am your daughter. But I am now a military wife.

IN MY SOLDIER'S EYES

In my soldier's eyes I see deep emotions
that words can never express.
Dark times are hidden behind those eyes
that sparkle when they smile.

In my soldier's eyes I see loss of innocence
that will never be regained.
Overwhelming experiences are disguised
with a wink of those eyes.

In my soldier's eyes I see secrets of past
fears that are never far from the heart's surface.
But, I also see a joy for life
that cannot be explained.

In my soldier's eyes I see a message that
says don't ask questions.
For the truths of war may never be revealed.

In my soldier's eyes I see things I will never know.

DREAMS OF HOME

I awoke with a smile on my face
For my dreams carried me to another time and place.
I smelled the sweet perfume of my true love
And heard the coo of a turtledove.

My sleep was deep and victory was near
The football team was scoring and the fans began to cheer.
The top was down on my faithful Ford
"He's back, he's home," was all I heard.

My dreams quickly faded and reality weighed in
Another day at war and sleep comes to an end.
I must dismiss distractions and tuck my dreams away
I must focus on fighting and pray our blood won't spill today.

War is a serious matter and focus is required
No time for dreams of home or other yearning desires.
The lives of many Marines depend solely on me
I must be the best as I was trained to be.

THERE IS NO WAR TODAY

I carry my son on my shoulders as we make
our way to our seats in the stands.
Today is a great day for baseball and I
will enjoy each moment that I can.

There is no war today

I sit quietly as the curtains on the stage are
raised to reveal twelve lovely girls.
Among the dancers is my pride and joy, my
daughter, who is the center of my world.

There is no war today

I hold her hand as we walk the path, speaking
of our future and whispering words of love.
As evening falls we rush home to a life
that is blessed by God above.

There is no war today

One day a war will come and I will gladly
go and stand as a warrior must.
I will fight for my family and a land I love, cherish and trust.

There is no war today

BEHIND THE GATE

Behind the gate the Stars and Stripes are
honored and patriotism abounds.

Behind the gate the privilege of rank is
a way of life understood by all.

Behind the gate the houses are alike and
the lawns are watered and manicured.

Behind the gate the dress code is no
mystery and is willingly adhered to.

Behind the gate ceremonies, parades, banquets,
and burials are carefully orchestrated.

Behind the gate is a world of rules, regulations,
orders, commands, codes, protocol, discipline,
love of God, family, and country.

You are welcome to visit, but you must take the
oath, to make your home behind the gate.

THE MARINE CORPS BALL

The stars on their shoulders brighten the night
The wings, bars, and stripes boast symbols of rank.
The shine on their medals a breathtaking sight
The Marine Corps Ball is tonight.

The ladies all glowing in beautiful gowns
As they enter the ballroom elegance abounds.
Majestic as a royal high court
The Marine Corps Ball is tonight.

The band plays a song as the gala commences
The ceremony commands everyone's attention.
A cake represents allegiance renewed
The Marine Corps Ball is tonight.

Formalities end and the dining begins
Followed by dancing and greeting old friends.
The night is exciting for all who attend
The Marine Corps Ball is tonight.

It's a celebration of grand proportion
With customs and traditions that are never broken.
Tomorrow may be just another day, but
The Marine Corps Ball is tonight.

WE LAUGHED AT THE SERGEANT MAJOR'S WIFE

We laughed at the Sergeant Major's wife.
What happened to her hair?
Is that all she has to wear?
Do her stockings have a tear?
Oh! We really shouldn't stare!

We laughed at the Sergeant Major's wife.
Didn't she wear that dress last year?
Are those real diamonds in her ears?
She's not up to standards, we fear!
Oh! Should we really even care?

We laughed at the Sergeant Major's wife.
She doesn't always know what to say.
She thinks she must get her way.
She'll come to our party, we pray.
Oh! We hope to be her some day!

BEST FRIENDS UNDER THE SUN

At a certain time in a special place,
Three families met on a military base.
These three families blended as one
Became best of friends under the sun.

Three military wives became best friends
And knew their friendship would never end.
Their children had lots of fun together
Their husbands embraced each other as brothers.

Together they dined, danced and played.
Together they cried, mourned and prayed.
Three families blended as one
Became best of friends under the sun.

Their lives were entwined for over two years,
Then one family got orders as they all had feared.
Now all the pieces seemed to fall apart
With nothing left but broken hearts.

But in matters of friendship one thing is true,
A best friend in life will always love you.
Three families blended as one
Remain best of friends under the sun.

MY BEST FRIEND IS A STRANGER

My best friend is a stranger
I met her yesterday.
We shared a pot of coffee
And talked the hours away.

We both live in base housing
Both our husbands went to war.
We've been looking for a friend
And we need not look anymore.

Now we're no longer strangers
We know each other well.
We've shared many secrets
That neither will ever tell.

If you're surrounded by strangers
On a base that's new to you.
It won't take long before a
Wife befriends you, too.

Once the friendship bond is woven
Between military wives.
You can rest assured and always know
You'll have a friend for life.

MOVING AGAIN

I had just become accustomed to living here.
Folks are friendly and I like my job.
The kids have friends.

Now we're moving again.
Between farewell potlucks and good-byes to friends
One thing is certain . . .

We will move again.

ODE TO MOVING

I've moved so many times
The moves get mixed up in my head
I pack, unpack and pack again
Is it moving or packing that I dread?

I've traveled far and traveled long
On water, land, by air
By train, by car, by plane, by van
I've lived life everywhere.

I toasted love in Paris, France
Sipped tea in London town
I drank the wines of Tuscany
My palate's made the rounds.

One child born in Omaha
Another born in Guam
The twins were born in Tennessee
Not certain where we're from.

I've moved from place to place to place
But in the scheme of life
Moving is just a routine part
Of being a military wife.

MOVING BLUES

Somewhere between receiving military orders to relocate
And actually arriving at a new location
A mood sets in.

Some call it the moving blues.

Looking at all your belongings
You wonder why you have so many things
And a mood sets in.

Some call it the moving blues.

You ask yourself why all the dishes
and glasses and ball gowns?
Are so many pairs of shoes necessary?
And a mood sets in.

Some call it the moving blues.

Eventually the household goods and personal effects
are packed, shipped and delivered
Leaving behind items deemed nonessential.
And a mood sets in.

Some call it the moving blues.

Somewhere between receiving military orders to relocate
And arriving at a new location
Even though it won't last forever
A mood sets in.

Some call it the moving blues.

NEVER GOOD-BYE

As we part you'll remain in my heart;

Farewell,

So Long,

Be Safe.

We'll blow a kiss, give a tender embrace;

Hurry Home,

See You Soon,

Take Care.

The rule unspoken,

Tradition never broken;

A tear is shed,

But good-bye is never said.

THE FOLKS BACK HOME

For years they watched you as you grew
When you had doubts they always knew.
You'd grow to be a brave, strong man
Who would leave home to protect our land.

They say prayers for you while you're away
And hope to see you home some day.
Some are the friends of your Mom and Dad
To some you're the child they never had.

You think of them from time to time
When thoughts of home cross your mind.
You wish you weren't so far away
But you're going home any day.

Their addresses remain the same
Their telephone numbers don't change.
No matter how far you roam
You'll always be welcomed
By the folks back home.

HOMEFRONT BLUES
(A letter from home)

The washer doesn't wash.
The dryer doesn't dry.
The oven doesn't broil.

The roof leaks.
The car stopped.
The dog ran away.

Junior broke his arm.
Shelly lost four teeth.
The sitter moved away.

Your parents stayed three weeks.
My parents stayed four.
We all got the flu.

We are doing okay.
Hope you are doing well.
See you soon.

A MILITARY CHRISTMAS

A military Christmas takes on many forms
surrounded by loved ones in the midst of harm
or maybe Christmas finds you in a foreign land
away from things familiar
perhaps a place with desert sand.

Are you spending Christmas Day
with family and friends back home
or maybe you'll be traveling
having dinner on the run?

One thing is true of Christmas
during peace time or in war
the peace and love of Christmas
finds your heart wherever you are.

THIS CHILD OF OURS

This Child Of Ours Has

Your Eyes,

Your Lips,

Your Hands,

Your Feet,

Your Hair,

Your Nose,

Your Smile.

This Child Of Ours Can't Wait

To Meet,

To Greet,

To Know,

To Love You.

(continued)

This Child Of Ours Is In

Your Heart,

Your Mind,

Your Soul,

Your Hopes,

Your Dreams.

This Child Of Ours Keeps Me

Bonded To You While You Are Away

This Child Of Ours Is Here

This Child Of Ours Is Us

MY MOTHER IS A SOLDIER

My mother is a soldier
Full of beauty, charm and grace;
I long to hold her hand again
And kiss her lovely face.

My mother is a soldier
She goes away to war;
She's always gone too long,
She's always gone too far.

My mother is a soldier
She's very brave and strong;
Daddy says she'll be home soon
To sing my goodnight song.

My mother is a soldier
She fights for you and me;
She risks her life in many ways
So we can all be free.

My mother is a soldier
But to me she is just Mom;
I know she thinks of me each day
Can't wait till she comes home.

FAREWELL, MY CHILD

I ask myself how I let you grow up so fast.

When was your diaper bag replaced with a sea bag?

When was your stroller replaced with an aircraft carrier?

When were your favorite jeans replaced
with a military uniform?

Where has the time gone?

Surely, I did not have enough time with you.

But, I must let you go.

Farewell, my child.

CAMOUFLAGE SUIT AND
BLACK SHINY BOOTS

On the hall closet door hangs his camouflage suit
placed neatly below it are his black shiny boots.
There's a big green sea bag packed at the door;
my Dad doesn't go to work any more.

Each day after school he's waiting for me
then we go inside and watch TV.
Sometimes he even drives me to school;
is this all real or an April Fool?

Mom's been cooking his favorite foods
Sometimes she seems in a melancholy mood.
Dad must be leaving but I don't know when;
He often leaves but comes home again.

Today Dad's not waiting or watching for me
I wonder if he's gone across the sea.
On the hall closet there's no camouflage suit,
no big green sea bag, no shiny black boots.

Months have passed since my Dad's been gone
one day soon I hope he'll be home.
As I enter the house I see shiny black boots;
on the hall closet hangs his camouflage suit.

WHEN MOMMY CRIES

When Mommy cries I hold her hand and
tell her everything will be okay
I don't mention that I know she's
crying because Daddy is away.

Instead, I say, "Mommy, I'm hungry," and
she dries her eyes and smiles
"Go into the kitchen," she says. "We'll
have dinner in a while."

I know she will cry again and I will hold her hand each time
When Daddy comes home he'll hold her hand and mine.
And everything will be okay.

WORKPLACE IN THE SKY

The sky is their workplace
They fly all around;
Their view of the world
Seen upside down.

The clouds are their cover
The stars are their friends;
They smile at the ground
When each flight ends.

Their need for adventure
Will never be quelled;
That's why they perform
Their duties so well.

Some call them crazy
Others understand;
The sky is their workplace
But they live on the land.

Their missions are many
They often fly alone;
They won't stop flying
Until the battle is won.

THE COMFORT OF A SEA BREEZE
(Poem for a Sailor's Wife)

Months have passed since your ship
sailed to a far away land.

I feel close to you walking along
the beach in the wet sand.

The gulls and other seabirds
watch as I pass them by.

I avoid looking in their eyes
for they might see me cry.

And then as the tears
from my eyes are about to fall.

A sea breeze caresses my cheek
and I know I'm not alone at all.

TALKING TO THE MOON ON STARRY NIGHTS

The moon shines from my sky
surrounded by twinkling stars.
I look up and smile, knowing that just hours ago
the moon and stars were visible in your sky.

Talking to the moon on starry nights
brings consolation and peace
because I know the moon will reveal its
beauty and light to you as night falls in your world.

So, look to the moon on starry nights,
my warrior, so far away,
and in your heart you will receive the
loving messages I send your way.

NO PEACE IN MY VALLEY

I find no peace in my valley.

I am alone with no one to hold.
My heart beats fast.
I shun all news of war.

I find no peace in my valley.

I am aware of my lifeless house.
My nerves are on edge.
I fear a knock at the door.

I find no peace in my valley.

I am a physical wreck.
My headaches no longer get relief.
Each day I ask, will I see my beloved again?

I find no peace in my valley.

STANDING TALL

I remember the silhouette of a tall
man in my bedroom doorway;
He stood erect dressed in his camouflage military uniform.

He walked towards my bed to tuck me in for the night;
He casts a shadow on the wall
from the shining light in the hall.

I felt at ease and knew I would sleep well that night;
For he struck fear in all monsters that
might dare invade my room.

Now the silhouette in my bedroom
doorway is of a brave man;
He sits erect in his wheelchair dressed in jeans and T-shirt.

He rolls his wheelchair towards my bed
to tuck me in for the night;
All monsters scatter as his shadow is cast
on the wall from the nightlight.

I will sleep well tonight because my Dad is home.
My hero has returned;
He still stands tall to me.

I'VE BEEN WHERE YOU'RE GOING

I walk through the valley in the shadow of evil eyes
I hear soft whispers behind my back.

Fake smiles are proudly displayed before me
False compliments pour like a waterfall over me.

I embrace the insincerity that is bestowed upon me
For most is due to curiosity and misunderstanding.

To dispel the rumors about who I am
I must reveal myself through my actions.

Only then will I be approached with
sincerity and truthfulness.

Only then can I make the path you must travel easier.

Only then will you understand that
I've been where you're going.

TRUE FRIENDS

We have been friends so long
I can't remember when I didn't know you.

We cried together during war.

We rejoiced together at births.

We mourned together at deaths.

We laughed together at ourselves.

We shared secrets long forgotten.

We burdened each other with troubles.

We showered each other with love.

We agreed to disagree.

We greeted each other with joy.

We bid each other farewell.

Even when we don't see each other for years
We are connected by experiences
Which remain fresh in our hearts.

PURPLE HEART

The Purple Heart recipient stands erect.
Although I know him as a friend
Today I recognize him as a hero.

Surrounded by friends, family, and comrades.
There is a bit of sadness in their eyes
But their pride shines through.

I look in his eyes and see a twinkle.
Do I witness a look of accomplishment
And a message of no regrets?

Just looking at him you know
He would gladly and willingly go
Engage the enemy in battle again.
His Purple Heart tells us so.

NO TEARS

It is a solemn occasion
A serviceman has been lost.
He's joined a band of brothers
Now part of a heavenly host.

On earth he left a partner
A lover, friend and wife.
She's delicate as a flower
Full of beauty, charm, and grace.

She sits with eyes straight forward
No expression on her face.
Surrounded by four children
A portrait of poise and grace.

As the gun salute is sounded
She tells herself, no tears.
In honor of her loved one
She conceals her private fears.

No tears, she whispers
As her husband's laid to rest.
Only dignity and pride are felt
For she knows he gave his best.

GOLD STAR TRIBUTE

Gold is precious and valuable
And so were the ones we lost.

With time others forget our pain
But for us the pain never fades.

As others enjoy their families
We are reminded each day of a void.

We feel only pride when we think of them
But they are still sorely missed.

We ask that you remember our loved ones
Who gave their lives for us.

Gold is precious and valuable
And so were the ones we lost.

OLD GLORY

It's not just a rag
It shouldn't be dragged
It's red, white and blue
For freedom tried and true,

Give Old Glory the respect it's due

When our flag is in view
You know what to do
Stand in its presence
Salute from the heart,

Give Old Glory the honor it's due

It can bring a tear to the eye
When seen flying high
It represents the pride
For which many have died,

Give Old Glory the reverence it's due

WE FLY THE FLAG

We fly the flag in cemeteries on Memorial Day
in memory of those who paid the ultimate cost.

We fly the flag in parades on Veterans' Day
to honor those who fought in battles won and lost.

We fly the flag along highways and byways
to remind us of things we value most.

We fly the flag throughout our land
in appreciation of the freedoms we so proudly boast.

SUNSET PARADE
(Eternal Rest)

The gun salute resonates.

The flag is folded.

Taps is played.

They are waiting and watching from above.

There will be a sunset parade in heaven.

Another hero will be welcomed into eternal rest.

RETIREMENT DAY

There is a sense of joy and sadness on this retirement day.
Thirty years is a long time, but seems
to have quickly passed.
A thirty-year military career is something to be proud of.
So friends, family and comrades-in-arms are
gathered to witness and to celebrate.

The Marine Corps retirement parade is
full of pomp and circumstance.
The precision of the marching band is
unmatched as band members glide
Across the perfectly maintained grass of the
parade field, their shoes shine like glass.
The melodious tunes resound throughout
the air, raising the level of patriotism
To an all time high among those who listen.

On this day the sky is blue, the sun shines
brightly and the birds keep a watchful eye.
The trees sway in the gentle breeze, the flag of
freedom waves and the ceremony begins.

The retiree stands tall and erect and is viewed
in a new light by family and friends.
Today he is a hero, saying farewell to
a life's work that he loves.
(continued)

RETIREMENT DAY *(continued)*

Some are wondering what he will do
after being a Marine for so long.
Others know he will always be a Marine
no matter where life takes him.

Speeches are made, commendations
given, a few tears are shed.
The troops pass in review as they honor
one who has served well.
The crowd is caught up in the pageantry and
feels a sense of pride and appreciation.
The band begins the Marine Corps Hymn as
all stand in recognition and tribute.

On this day the sky is blue, the sun shines
brightly and the birds keep a watchful eye.
The trees sway in the gentle breeze, the flag
of freedom waves as the ceremony ends.

The troops extend well wishes and reflect
on wars fought and times gone by.
Officers and senior staff members look at the
retiree as though seeing the future,
For they know the day is coming when they
too, will say farewell to the Corps.
But today they bid farewell to a comrade who
has lived up to the standards of valor.

(continued)

The Marine's family recalls the times they
were connected only by prayers.
They remember when letters, packages, and
photographs were necessary reminders
That he was not forgotten while far away from
those he loved and missed the most.
His wife and children see the man they have waited
for so many times coming home to stay.

On this day the sky is blue, the sun shines
brightly and the birds keep a watchful eye.
The trees sway in the gentle breeze, the flag
of freedom waves as a new life beckons.

About The Author

Margaret Roberts has experienced military life firsthand. Married to a retired United States Marine Corps Sergeant Major, Roberts resided most of her husband's active duty career in the California desert and developed a respect for the desert environment. Her first book of poems is evidence of her fascination with desert flowers and she compares them and their survival to the military lifestyle, particularly the life of a military wife. Desert Flowers: Poems of Love and Life is a labor of love that will be enjoyed by all who read it. Roberts is a retired government employee now residing in Florida with her husband. She has a daughter, son-in-law, and two grandsons.